THE
MINDFULNESS
JOURNAL

THE MINDFULNESS JOURNAL

An Hachette UK Company
www.hachette.co.uk

Vie Books, an imprint of Summersdale Publishers Ltd
Part of Octopus Publishing Group Limited
Carmelite House
50 Victoria Embankment
LONDON
EC4Y 0DZ
UK

www.summersdale.com

Printed and bound in the Czech Republic

ISBN: 978-1-78783-304-3

Substantial discounts on bulk quantities of Summersdale books are available to corporations, professional associations and other organizations. For details contact general enquiries: +44 (0) 1243 756902 or email: enquiries@summersdale.com.

THIS JOURNAL BELONGS TO …

_____

INTRODUCTION

Mindfulness is about focusing on the magic of the present moment. Rather than fretting about the past or worrying about the future, the aim is to experience life as it unfolds moment by moment. This simple practice is immensely powerful. As we rush through our lives, mindfulness encourages us to stop constantly striving for something new or better and to embrace acceptance and gratitude. This allows us to tap into the joy and wonder in our lives, and to listen to the wisdom of our hearts. This journal will show you how to experience small but beautiful moments of mindfulness every day and so guide you along the path to finding more peace and contentment in your life. As well as mindful exercises, this journal offers the space for you to write down or doodle your thoughts and feelings freely. Revisit your completed pages whenever you are seeking a moment of calm and reflection.

A LITTLE BIT
OF MINDFULNESS
EVERY DAY

A NEW DAY BEGINS.

A Refreshing Way
to Start the Day

On waking in the morning, rather than springing out of bed to start your busy day, spend a few moments becoming aware of your surroundings. Listen to the sounds around you and notice what thoughts are in your mind. Sit up straight, place your feet on the floor, and tune in to your body. Focus on your breathing and allow your stomach to rise and fall. Imagine that you are breathing in the morning light. Visualize each breath flooding your body with golden light from the rising sun. Feel energized, ready for the day ahead.

Use the circles below to note down some thoughts that you'd like to reflect on in these first few moments of the day.

LET YOUR STRESSES FLOAT AWAY

Visualization can be a powerful meditation tool. If you are feeling anxious, visualize a hot air balloon and imagine that you are putting all your stress and negativity into the balloon. Then watch it gently float away into the distance, taking your worries and concerns with it.

If you're new to visualization then start by writing your worries in the hot air balloon on the opposite page. Picture the balloon floating off the page and up, up, up and away.

What a benediction is this fragrance of the early morning!

Sarah Smiley

INSTRUCTION FOR LIFE:

PAY ATTENTION.

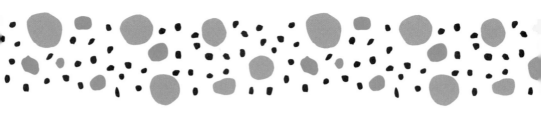

Get Started

Mindfulness is not something you achieve overnight; it is a habit which is developed gradually over time.

Start by picking one or two opportunities to treat with a mindful attitude every day. You might decide to be mindful every time you brush your teeth, walk to the car, open a door or make a cup of tea, for example. Whichever action you choose, make sure you give your whole attention to it. When you open a door, watch your hand grasp the doorknob, feel the weight of the door as you pull it open, and hear the sounds of whatever is on the other side of the doorway... If you do this every time you open a door, you will be amazed at how automatic this process becomes. This simple ritual will allow mindfulness to establish a foothold in your life. All you need to do is take baby steps and commit to being mindful for a few seconds several times a day.

Digital detox

The non-stop stream of information we receive from mobiles, computers and TVs can be overwhelming. It's a good idea to give our mental "inbox" a break from time to time. Turn off your devices, hide all gadgets and give yourself some time off from the endless technological invasion in your life.

Learn the right technique

You can learn mindfulness in numerous ways to suit your preferences and budget. If you're an auditory learner, you could buy a mindfulness CD or podcast to guide you into a meditative state. If you prefer to learn directly from a teacher, consider signing up to a local introductory class or investing in some one-to-one tuition. Many yoga courses and retreats also include mindfulness meditation as part of the curriculum. Learning in a group has the benefit of a strong atmosphere of community and friendship, but if you prefer to learn in the privacy of your own home, try taking an online course such as the one at www.bemindful.co.uk.

Use visual cues

Being mindful is not difficult to do – it's the remembering that's the key! Place inspiring pictures and notes around your home to remind you and your family to "be mindful", "pause" and "take a breath". These visual triggers can be all you need to snap you back to the present moment.

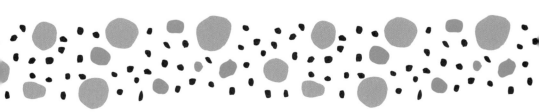

Whatever the present
moment contains, accept it
as if you had chosen it.

Eckhart Tolle

FORGIVE AND FORGET

Open your heart and soul to
forgiveness, both for yourself and
others. Holding on to resentment
or anger only fuels other negative
emotions. Be open to healing and love.

Things to Be Grateful for

Use this page to list all the positive things in your life – from the small things that make you smile, such as the view from your window, to the bigger things, such as your health or your family.

- ○ _____
- ○ _____
- ○ _____
- ○ _____
- ○ _____
- ○ _____
- ○ _____
- ○ _____
- ○ _____
- ○ _____
- ○ _____

- ○ _____
- ○ _____
- ○ _____
- ○ _____
- ○ _____
- ○ _____
- ○ _____
- ○ _____
- ○ _____
- ○ _____
- ○ _____

Everyday Mindfulness

Many of us go through our daily routines on autopilot, barely noticing what we are doing. An easy way to focus your attention on the present moment is to focus on simple tasks. For instance, make your bed with 100 per cent focus and attention each morning so you create a calm transition from bedroom and sleep to the outside world and the rest of your day. Similarly, when cleaning your teeth or brushing your hair, notice every sensory detail.

Draw yourself completing one of your morning tasks. Try to include all the details you noticed, such as the pattern on your bedspread or the smell of mint as you brushed your teeth. Label anything you can't capture in images.

The greatest step toward
a life of simplicity is
to learn to let go.

Steve Maraboli

SEE THE GOOD EVERYWHERE.

Happiness is a Journey, not a Destination.

BREATHE INTO TENSION

If you encounter a difficult
situation today, notice which
parts of your body feel tense,
then breathe into the area to
help you relax. Draw circles
around this text as you breathe,
adding embellishments at
the moment your lungs are
fullest and the moment you've
expelled all your breath.

THE ORDINARY CAN BE

EXTRAORDINARY

Stand firm, like a tree

A great way to ground yourself when you're in the midst of turmoil is to take some deep breaths and visualize roots growing from your feet into the ground. Stand firm like a tree, while the chaos around you blows through your branches and disappears on the breeze.

Draw roots growing from the shoes opposite and use this as a visualization tool.

In the midst of movement and chaos, keep stillness inside of you.

Deepak Chopra

The most important thing
about being mindful

is remembering to be mindful.

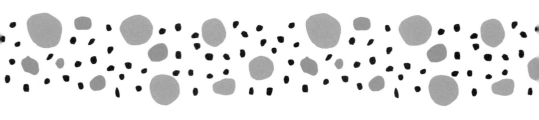

Ordinary into Extraordinary

Take a daily routine activity, such as taking a shower, and be curious and alert about yourself, noticing every sensory detail. Notice if you're thinking ahead to what you're doing next and, if so, gently bring your attention back to the present.

Calm reading

Notice today how you scan over most of your reading material. Slow down and read with your full attention, absorbing the full meaning of the words and not skipping sections. How different does this feel from usual? Does it make you feel more relaxed? Do the words affect you more deeply?

Make more memories

Don't take things for granted. Everyday moments, when experienced fully, can become lifelong memories – from savouring the first freshly picked strawberries of the season or the blackbird's song outside your window to holding a new-born child.

Arrive mindfully

Whenever you arrive somewhere, give yourself a moment to "check in". Become aware of how your body is feeling – especially any aches and tensions. Take note of what emotions you are carrying. Acknowledge all of this, taking no more than a minute, and you will be centred and present, ready to move on with your day.

Stay grounded

When you're in a rush – dashing around the supermarket or taking the dog for a quick walk – bring your awareness to your feet. Slow down slightly and feel your feet connect you to the ground. This will help you to gain a sense of equilibrium and balance.

Don't jump to conclusions

There is great truth in the familiar saying, "Don't judge a book by its cover." We often prejudge people by their appearance or the sound of their voice. Being mindful means seeing everything in the present moment, without leaping to unfounded conclusions.

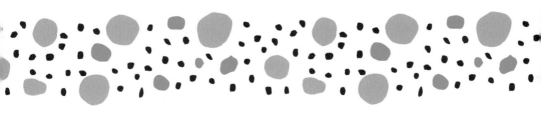

PAUSE

IT'S WHAT GIVES YOU YOUR POWER.

YOU ALWAYS HAVE A CHOICE
IN HOW TO RESPOND.

Choose Your Reaction

Write down a sentence describing an incident that you had a negative emotional reaction to, whether it was sadness, anger or fear. Then draw several concentric circles around the sentence. In the ring nearest to the centre, write your initial emotions. Write the feelings and thoughts you experienced after some time passed in the second ring, and then in the third ring, and so on, tracking the development of your emotions over time.

Strong emotions, such as anger, hurt or fear, can erupt very quickly. But there's usually a split second in which you can pause before you react. When you feel something inside you being triggered, become mindful of your breath. Notice the sensations in your body. Realize you have a choice about what you do next before you react.

LET GO OF THE

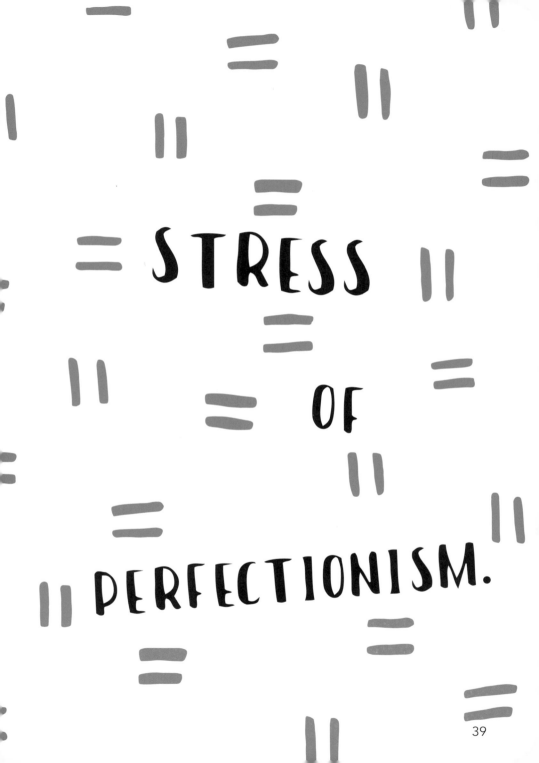

STRESS OF PERFECTIONISM.

Connect with People

Take time out to sit on a bench or a window seat in a cafe
and watch people go by. Don't read, talk or catch up on
social media — just people-watch. Feel connected to everyone
and watch them with an open mind and compassion.

**Use the space here to write words that best
describe some of the people you see walking by.**

Stick with It

Developing a daily mindfulness practice takes patience
and determination. It can be hard work to keep pulling
your mind back to the present moment. There may
be times when you want to throw in the towel, but
be determined. If you persevere, you will learn from

_____

_____

_____

_____

_____

_____

_____

_____

_____

_____

_____

_____

_____

_____

obstacles and overcome them. Your ability will improve and the benefits will start to become more obvious. You will start to feel more present, peaceful and alive.

Note down instances when you've been determined and practised mindfulness.

Whenever you feel your patience wavering, remind yourself that mindfulness works like a muscle — the more you exercise it, the stronger it gets.

The more we notice
things to appreciate,
the more they
seem to grow.

The mind… can be compared
to the sky, covered by
layers of cloud which
hide its true nature.

Kalu Rinpoche

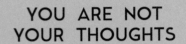

YOU ARE NOT
YOUR THOUGHTS

Do your thoughts overwhelm and confuse you? Do you wish your mind had an "off" button? We identify with our thoughts and allow them to dictate how we feel. As our thoughts are often "noisy", negative and chaotic, it's no wonder we struggle. The solution lies not in trying to get rid of our thoughts altogether but in stopping our habit of identifying with them. Simply observe your thoughts without judgement and let them go.

Start the process of letting your negative thoughts go by writing them on the page opposite and then crossing them out.

Accept people for
who they are,

including yourself!

There is No Destination

When we embark on a new project, we normally have a goal or destination in mind. The beauty of mindfulness is that it is a process; there is no end destination. You cannot exist outside of the present moment. Life is what is happening to you right now. So the only goal when practising mindfulness is to be fully present.

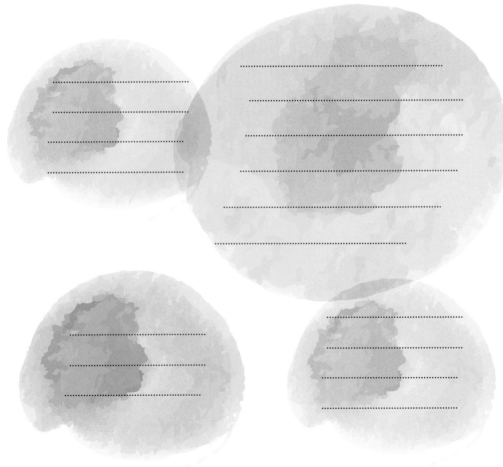

Try writing mindfulness mantras in the bubbles
below and read them regularly. An example
mantra is: There is nowhere more important
for me to be than right here, right now.

....

....

....

....

....

....

....

....

....

....

....

....

....

....

....

....

The greatest weapon against
stress is our ability to choose
one thought over another.

William James

Mindfulness
is seeing
things with
fresh eyes.

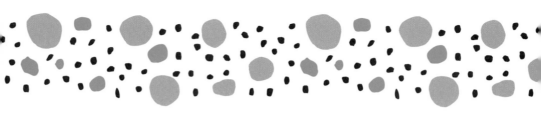

Be Kind to Yourself

Always be compassionate and kind, especially toward yourself. You're still getting to grips with mindfulness practice and it's important to view mistakes and setbacks as part of the learning process.

Stop assuming the worst

If your mind is racing and you are consumed with worry, are you scaring yourself with "what-ifs"? What-ifs and imagined scenarios may seem incredibly real but they are a figment of our imagination. A large proportion of the things we imagine never actually happen. Let's say you take your cat to the vets because he has stopped eating and you spend the day before the appointment worrying that the vet will discover a terrible disease. In reality, the vet finds a splinter in your cat's gum and removes it, solving the problem. Yet you spent the previous day gripped with anxiety. If worrying is controlling your life, it's time to take control. The second you realize you are dwelling on a worst-case scenario, bring yourself back to the present. Remind yourself that you are not a fortune teller! Worrying serves no purpose other than to make you feel anxious. Focus on the facts of a situation and on what is (rather than what-ifs!).

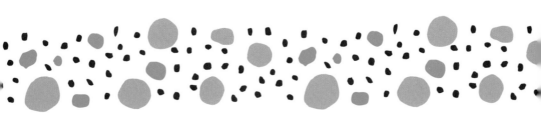

Notice what distracts you

We each have unique tendencies or thoughts that pull us away from the present moment. Start paying attention to your thoughts and jot down the types of thoughts that distract you most often. Do you have a tendency to dwell on the past or the future? Are you consumed with thoughts of guilt, fear, regret or worry? Do you ruminate on achieving perfection or success, wealth and recognition? Writing these tendencies down can help you become more mindful about what is going on in your head when you stray from the present moment. This insight can lead you to mindfulness.

Forgive yourself

Self-compassion is essential when learning mindfulness. You will not be able to sustain mindfulness 100 per cent of the time. You may be "too busy" to practise or forget to practise altogether. You may be unable to stop your mind from wandering, or you may find yourself thinking about being mindful rather than practising being mindful! The ability to forgive yourself at these times is crucial. Self-compassion will enable you to pick yourself up, dust yourself off and try again. If you beat yourself up every time you falter, you will be far less likely to stick to the kind of regular practice which will impact on your health and happiness.

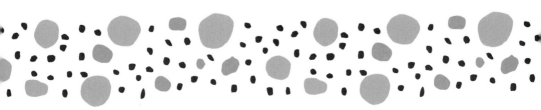

COME HOME TO THE PRESENT.

We have only now, only
this single eternal moment
opening and unfolding
before us, day and night.

Jack Kornfield

Give in to
Your Creativity

Try something creative – draw or paint a
picture on this page, right now.

Don't worry about the quality of what you're
producing, and don't hold back – the most
important thing is to immerse yourself in the
joy of creating! If you're not sure of what to
draw, draw what you see in front of you.

Immerse Yourself in Music

Listening to music can be a great mindfulness exercise. Choose music that is soothing: instrumental or classical are good choices. Begin by sitting with a comfortable, upright posture. Choose a space where you can minimize any outer distractions and be sure to turn off your phone, computer

and television. Spend a few moments breathing fully and completely, immersing yourself in your inhalation and exhalation. As you begin to listen to the music, focus on the sound and vibration of each note. Notice any feelings that the music conjures up for you and any sensations that occur in your body as you listen. If other thoughts creep into your head, gently bring your attention back to the music.

Fill in one of the circles below using a colour that suits your mood and the tone and emotion of the piece you were listening to.

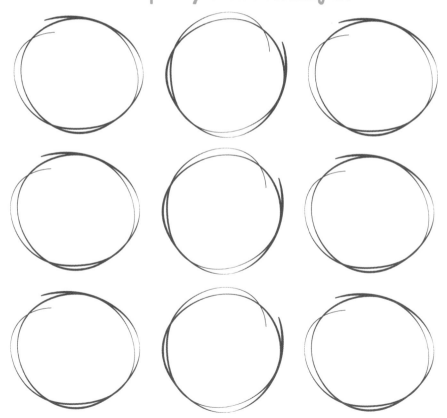

Be Open to New Experiences

When travelling to a new place, it is easy to get distracted by taking photographs and buying souvenirs. Make sure you get the most out of the experience by bringing your presence and

_____

_____

_____

_____

_____

_____

_____

_____

_____

_____

_____

_____

_____

_____

_____

_____

_____

full attention to all that you experience. Savour the sights, sounds and smells of your new location.

Write a short description of your arrival at a new location. Include your experiences of all five senses, including textures, sounds and tastes.

_____

_____

_____

_____

_____

_____

_____

_____

_____

_____

_____

_____

_____

_____

_____

LOOK FOR THINGS TO BE THANKFUL FOR.

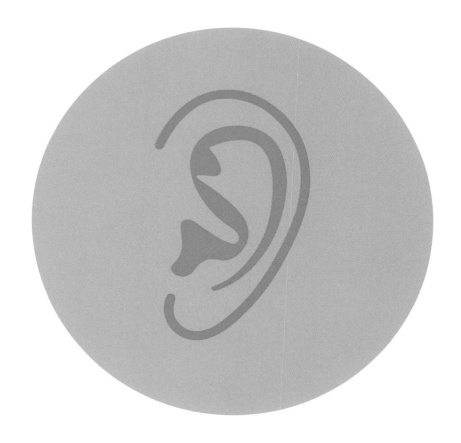

Put your ear down close to
your soul and listen hard.

Anne Sexton

Try Something New

You are instinctively being mindful whenever your brain is engaged in something unfamiliar. So make it your goal to try new things from time to time, whether that's learning a musical instrument or going to an art class. If you feel anxiety,

fear or resistance when facing a new activity, mindfully
notice that you are experiencing fear of the unknown.

**Jot down a list of things you've always wanted
to try, whether it's skydiving or a salsa class. By
slowly building confidence you can enjoy new hobbies
and experience more moments of mindfulness.**

○ _____   ○ _____

○ _____   ○ _____

○ _____   ○ _____

○ _____   ○ _____

○ _____   ○ _____

○ _____   ○ _____

○ _____   ○ _____

○ _____   ○ _____

○ _____   ○ _____

○ _____   ○ _____

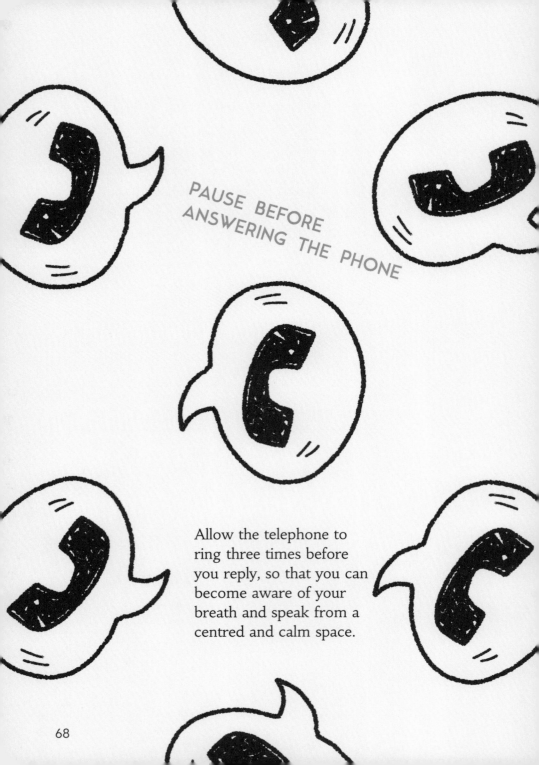

PAUSE BEFORE
ANSWERING THE PHONE

Allow the telephone to
ring three times before
you reply, so that you can
become aware of your
breath and speak from a
centred and calm space.

Life happens.
Let it be.

Get Dressed Mindfully

As you get dressed and undressed, slow the process down and observe whether your movements are comfortable and flowing.

or hasty and rushed. Notice the textures and fabrics
of your clothes and how they feel on your skin.

**Draw swatches of your clothes, including the
pattern and grain of the material. Try to capture
the visual impression of the material's texture.**

An awake heart
is like a sky that
pours light.

Hāfez

MAKE
TODAY
A
"NO RUSH"
DAY.

Tune in to Your Body

The next time you seek out a sugary snack, stop and think about how you are feeling. People often turn to food in an attempt to self-soothe or deal with stressful situations. Recognize that you are looking for something to eat that you think will bring you satisfaction.

Sit down and be fully present with this craving. Draw a fruit bowl filled with the things you really need, like a night dedicated to working on a creative project or a walk by the seaside.

Recipes

Use the following pages to write down your favourite soothing recipes, so that you always have some tasty food ideas on hand when you feel you need to take a step back and reflect.

Recipes

Recipes

_____
_____
_____
_____
_____
_____
_____
_____
_____
_____
_____
_____
_____
_____
_____
_____
_____
_____
_____
_____

Recipes

Do a "Body Sweep"

Research shows that our emotions manifest in our body.
For example, negative emotions often cause people to tense
the muscles in their jaw and around their eyes and mouth.
With repeated stress, these muscles can become sore
and tight. One of the key ways to balance your mind-body
connection is to stop and give yourself a "body sweep".

**Sit quietly and systematically scan your body, starting at
the top of your head and moving down over your face,
the back of your head, your shoulders, arms, hands, torso,
hips, legs and feet. As you do this, notice the sensations
you feel. Are there any areas of tension, pressure or
discomfort? If so, colour them in on the body opposite
and then breathe into these areas and allow them to
soften and relax. It may also help to label parts of
the body where you experience tension frequently, so
you know where you need to place the most focus.**

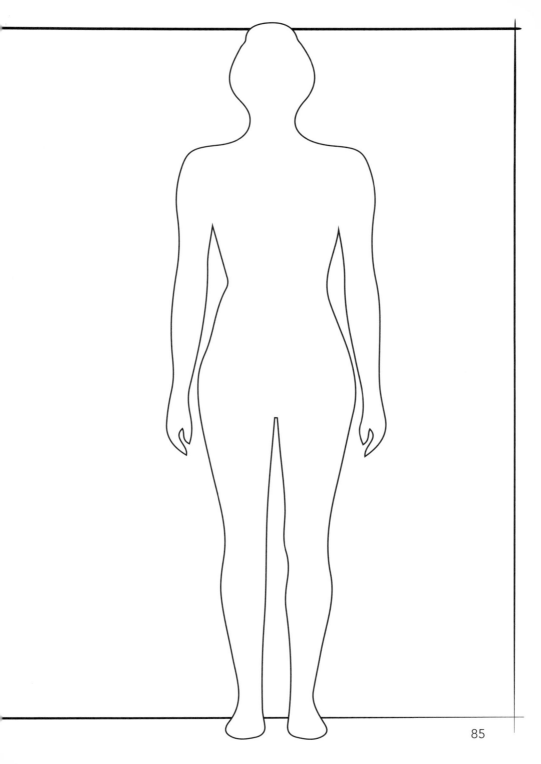

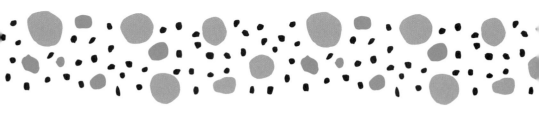

Listen to Your Body

It's important to take note of what your body tells you,
and to respond to what it wants. Allow your body to be
your guide and always remember to look after it.

Practise mindful listening

We often find that when we listen to others we are concentrating on what to say next, filling up our minds with our own opinions or even speaking out of turn. Try listening with mindfulness – hear the person without judgement or the need to immediately express a view. Be aware that the word "listen" can be shuffled around to spell "silent".

Breathe into your body

Take a moment to "belly breathe" for a greater flow of oxygen and instant calm. Breathe in deeply, allowing your stomach to rise outward. On the out-breath, allow your stomach to fall back.

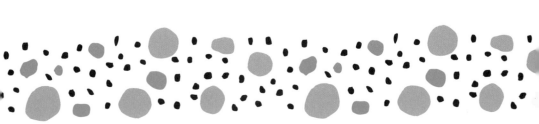

Go barefoot

Going barefoot is good for our health and it's the perfect opportunity to practise mindfulness. Spend the day barefoot at home today and enjoy feeling the texture and temperature beneath your feet as you move from room to room. If you have a garden, venture outside and focus on the soft grass beneath your feet.

Take advantage of queues

Turn inconvenient moments in your day into opportunities for mindfulness. If you're stuck in a queue at the supermarket or in a traffic jam, become aware of how your body, posture and thoughts are affected by the situation.

Take a power shower

Transform your shower or bath by bringing your full attention to the experience. Feel the warm water against your skin and listen to the sound it makes. Savour the scent of the soap and shampoo and be aware of the variety of textures beneath your hands. Imagine that you are washing yourself clean of any negativity.

Are you sitting mindfully?

Bring your awareness to your chair or the ground and become aware of pressures against your body and textures on your skin. Shift your weight to give you greater comfort and notice any areas of tension such as shoulders, lower back or neck.

Breathe in Calm

Wherever you are, you can incorporate a calm, breathing meditation into your day. Start by becoming aware of your breath as it enters and leaves your nostrils. Breathe to your own rhythm. After a few breaths, focus on breathing in and breathing out the feelings you wish to nurture:

_____

_____

_____

_____

_____

_____

_____

_____

_____

_____

_____

_____

_____

I BREATHE IN LOVE. I BREATHE OUT LOVE.

I BREATHE IN STRENGTH. I BREATHE OUT STRENGTH.

I BREATHE IN HARMONY. I BREATHE OUT HARMONY.

Create as many lines to your meditation as you wish, using words that are meaningful to you and the situation you find yourself in. This meditation is especially helpful if you're about to do something you feel nervous about: a job interview, a meeting with your child's teacher or any other important task.

The time to be
happy is now,
the place to be
happy is here.

Robert G. Ingersoll

It's good to have an
end in mind, but in
the end what counts
is how you travel.

Orna Ross

Mindful Movement

Mindful exercise is about performing physical activity
while focusing inward. This allows you to get more in
touch with your body. The idea is to let go of distractions
and unrelated thoughts, and focus your attention
on your breath, movements and sensations. If you

do this while working out, you will enhance your enjoyment, decrease your chances of injury, and even improve the efficacy of the exercise you're doing. Most importantly, it will help you develop a healthy and loving relationship with your body.

Use this page to note down some of your favourite exercises, and write out how it makes you feel when you move mindfully.

Remember, you're aiming for quality, not quantity. Try turning off your gadgets and bringing your attention to your breath and your movements while you are jogging, cycling, rowing or lifting weights.

BY BEING
HAPPY IN THIS
MOMENT

YOU ARE
CREATING MORE
HAPPINESS.

Getting from A to B

As you walk from one place to another, become aware of your posture. Notice if you are rushing ahead, with your shoulders hunched with tension. Straighten your spine and lift your chest and be aware of your connection to the ground as each foot is placed in front of the other. Enjoy being alert and mindful while you walk. Throughout your day, take every opportunity to walk with peace and serenity – when walking to your car, moving from room to room at home or at work, or while out shopping, bring your full presence to the process of walking and you will glide serenely through your day.

Ask a friend to snap a picture of you in profile as you practise mindful walking. Print them and stick them in here to track your improved posture.

You are

exactly

where

you need
to be.

Mindful Eating

If you regularly wolf down your food without really tasting it, start practising mindfulness whenever you eat. As you prepare your food, savour every culinary aroma. When you sit down to eat, take a moment to quietly give thanks for the

_____

_____

_____

_____

_____

_____

_____

_____

_____

_____

_____

_____

_____

_____

_____

food in front of you. As you eat your meal, focus all your attention on the tastes, sounds, smells and sensations you are experiencing, rather than anything else going on around you.

Keep a food journal and describe the sensations you experienced during your mindful eating.

_____

_____

_____

_____

_____

_____

_____

_____

_____

_____

See if turning the TV or radio off and eating in silence makes you appreciate the food and the feeling of being full more than usual. Try placing your fork down in-between mouthfuls and chewing each mouthful slowly in order to relish every taste sensation.

LIKE CLOUDS
IN THE SKY,

EVERYTHING
IS IN A
CONSTANT
PROCESS OF
CHANGE.

Smile Throughout Your Body

If you are feeling a little low, try this healing smile meditation.
Bring to mind someone or something that makes you smile
or laugh – your best friend, your pet or your partner, for
example. Soak in the warm feeling you get when you think about
them and let the corners of your mouth curl up into a gentle
smile. Let this smile gather joy and energy and breathe these

good feelings into your heart. On each out breath, direct this warm, happy glow around your body. Let it travel to all your organs – your lungs, heart, liver, kidneys and digestive system. Smile into each of them. Smile, and let this loving energy travel along your limbs – along your arms, hands, legs and feet. Keep visualizing what makes you feel happy. Breathe it into your heart and keep radiating this happiness out around your body.

Practise this healing smile meditation any time you are going through a rough patch or are having a bad day. Draw a happy face below every time you complete this ritual.

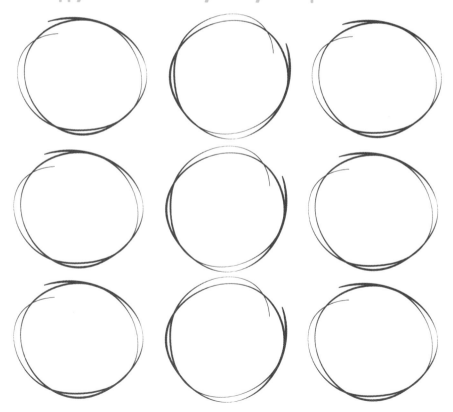

Affirm It, Believe It

Affirmations are quiet reminders that you repeat to yourself, either during your meditation or as you go about your day. They can be particularly helpful if you find you are stuck in a negative thought loop. Choose an affirmation that has meaning for you, such as, "Everything that is happening now is happening for my ultimate good" or "I am at peace with the world".

Write your affirmations below.

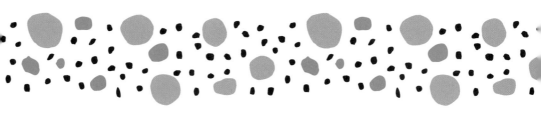

Take a Break

Use mindfulness to help you reduce the
unwanted distractions in your life and allow
you to focus on what really matters.

Conquer information overload

Reduce the amount of information you consume. Cancel subscriptions for magazines you barely have time to read and unsubscribe from catalogues, junk mail and emails. A cluttered mind is a stressed mind. Free up your mind and make space to listen to the whispers of your heart and soul.

Meditate to switch off stress

The more frequently you worry, the more your sympathetic nervous system kicks in. This triggers your "fight or flight" response – stress hormones are released into the bloodstream, heart rate increases, muscles contract and blood pressure rises. To reduce this stress response, you can consciously turn on the parasympathetic nervous system, which restores your body to a state of calm.

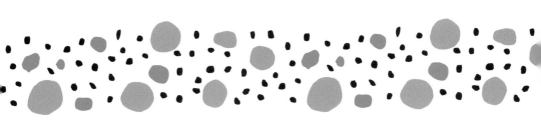

Meditation is excellent for this — simply sit and focus on some deep, slow breaths. Be aware of each inhalation and exhalation. Notice the movement of your body as you breathe and if your mind throws up distractions, gently bring it back to your breath. Within a few minutes, you will feel back in balance, fully alert for your next tasks.

Stop the clock!

Plan a mindful weekend without clocks or watches. Listen to your body instead — you choose when to get up, when to eat, what tasks you feel like doing and the length of time you spend on them.

Do less, notice more

Instead of cramming as much as possible into your day, do less and do it more slowly, more fully and with more concentration. Take the time to luxuriate in whatever activity you're doing, whether you're cooking supper or chatting to a friend. You should find the experience relaxing and fulfilling when you're not rushing through tasks.

Let thoughts come and go

Many people think that the goal of meditation is to achieve a blank mind, with no thoughts at all, but having thoughts while you meditate is perfectly normal. In fact, it's what's supposed to happen! Dealing with thoughts is how mindfulness meditation works. When you notice that you are distracted by your thoughts, gently bring your attention back to the object of your meditation. Over time, this simple practice will change how you relate to distractions, and increase your ability to focus and concentrate.

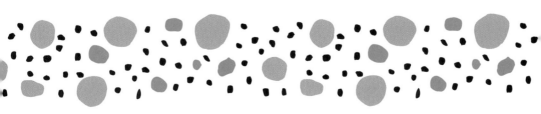

Meditation practice
isn't about trying
to throw ourselves
away or become
something better. It's
about befriending
who we are already.

Pema Chödrön

The real
meditation is how
you live your life.

Jon Kabat-Zinn

MAGICAL MANDALAS

Mandalas are geometric designs with a circular pattern that are used for meditation, prayer and healing. They have been used for thousands of years in the Buddhist and Hindu traditions as meditational tools to clear the mind. They have also been used in many therapeutic environments to help people unearth feelings that need to be expressed. Mandalas can be used in several ways. Creating your own mandala can facilitate your personal growth; helping you become more conscious of your inner thoughts and allowing you to tap into your creativity, without the need for any artistic expertise. You can also use mandalas to enhance your meditation practice. Colour in the mandala opposite and let your mind be absorbed by the patterns and colours you see. This soothes the busy, chattering mind and allows the creative mind to break free.

Breathe. Let go.
And remind yourself
that this very moment is
the only one you know
you have for sure.

Oprah Winfrey

Drink your tea slowly and reverently, as if it is the axis on which the world earth revolves.

Thích Nhất Hạnh

Be Thankful

It's easy to get swept away by negative thinking and overlook what is really important. One way to be more positive in your life is to be thankful. People who have a strong sense of gratitude are happier and healthier than those who don't. Be thankful for your body and

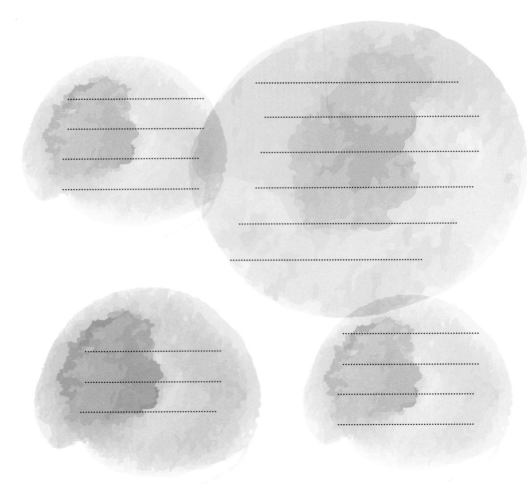

the things it is capable of – hands that let you do so much, legs that take you to so many places, eyes that see the beauty in the world, and heart and lungs constantly working for your survival. This is a far healthier approach than focusing on the body parts you don't like or that are less than perfect in your opinion!

Write the things you are thankful for below – your health, your loved ones, your dog, the sound of laughter or a beautiful summer's day.

....

....

....

....

....

....

....

....

....

....

....

....

....

....

....

....

Light a Candle

Light a candle and place it on the table before you eat. This brings calm and peace to a setting, alleviates tension and encourages people to eat more slowly and thoughtfully.

After you've finished eating, watch the candle; note the way the light flickers and the shadows that it creates. Draw your impression of them here.

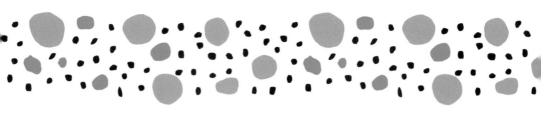

Be Happy, Don't Worry

Positivity is key to a mindful existence. Use these mindfulness tips to find your positive and joyful path through life.

Good news

Decide that from now on you will stop spreading bad news and only share good! Read something positive before you go to sleep at bedtime, and repeat this affirmation to yourself at regular intervals: "My thoughts are filled with positivity and my life is brimming with happiness."

Childlike wonder

Young children are constantly curious. They see the magic in everyday things – a spider, a buttercup or bubbles in the bath. They teach us to stop and look again, with amazement, at what is in front of us. Start viewing the world through a child's eyes and see how it brightens up your day!

Namaste

The Sanskrit greeting "Namaste" means "the light in me greets the light in you". On waking today, decide that you will look for the secret goodness in three people you deal with. Open your heart as you speak with them and notice how this intention affects your thoughts, and the interaction you have with them.

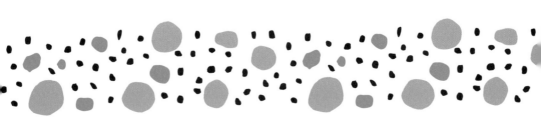

You are not alone

When you find yourself caught up in a tangle of negative thoughts, place your hand on your heart. See if you can feel it beating and notice how your chest rises and falls with every breath. Think of all the heartbeats doing the same thing across the world, then move on with a renewed sense of shared experience.

Practise acceptance

Our natural tendency is to resist painful thoughts or feelings. This means we suffer two "pains" – the painful situation itself and our resistance to it! For example, you feel stressed because of an impending deadline at work and think, "I hate feeling so stressed". The primary pain is stress about your workload. The secondary pain is feeling "I wish I wasn't so stressed". The solution is acceptance. Let the unpleasant situation or emotion be as it is, without trying to change it or push it away. By fighting the pain ("I hate feeling like this, I need this pain to go away") you intensify your suffering. If you accept your feelings, however, you don't heap an extra layer of pain upon the pain you are already feeling. Acceptance doesn't mean you like what is happening; it just means you accept that certain things are beyond your control. No matter what the situation, resisting the situation and feelings only magnifies the pain.

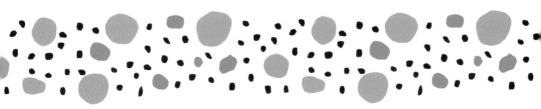

The Sound of Water

Science has proven that "blue space" including seas, rivers and lakes can positively affect our well-being. The sight, sound, smell and feel of water calms our frazzled minds and bodies. For this reason, water is a great aid to practising mindfulness. The next time you are in a "blue space", put your worries to one side and focus instead on the physical sensations you are experiencing – the sound of crashing waves, the smell of salt in the air, the cool water against your skin or the ripples of a bubbling stream. This relaxing exercise will help you to focus on the present moment and achieve a sense of inner quietness.

Describe your experience in the "blue space" in words or pictures on these pages.

SEEK TO
EXPAND YOUR

HEART

NOT YOUR
POSSESSIONS.

LET NATURE NURTURE YOU

Get up a few minutes early and give yourself time to take a gentle stroll in a quiet, calming space before heading to work. Take note of the plants and flowers you spot along the way, appreciating the beauty of nature around you.

BIRDWATCHING

We are surrounded by birds, but how often do we stop to notice them? Place water outside for the birds – and stop to watch them wash and preen their feathers. Pay close attention to the soundtrack of birdsong that accompanies you as you go about your day.

Draw the birds in flight or enjoying the water.

LOOK AT EVERYTHING AS THOUGH YOU WERE SEEING IT FOR THE FIRST TIME.

When you realize there is
nothing lacking, the whole
world belongs to you.

Lao Tzu

Focus on a Flower

Flowers are beautiful objects, but how often do you pause to really drink in their beauty? The next time you're outside, let your gaze settle on a flower. Take in its pure, bright colour

and soft, velvety petals, and inhale its delicate fragrance. See its beauty and intricacy, and place all other thoughts to one side while you marvel at the detail of this natural wonder.

Draw snapshots of the flower such as the pattern on its petal or a close up of its stamen or leaf.

Colour Therapy

Look around you and focus on the colours that you see.
Let your eyes wander as you absorb the hues of purple
sunsets, yellow pumpkins, ruby berries or the slate-grey sea.

**Pick out all the colours of the view in front
of you and colour the circles in accordingly.**

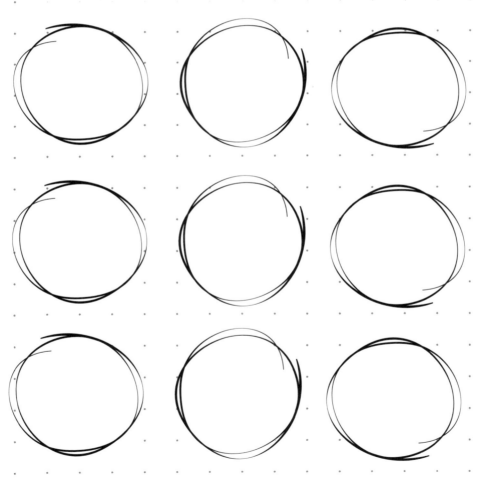

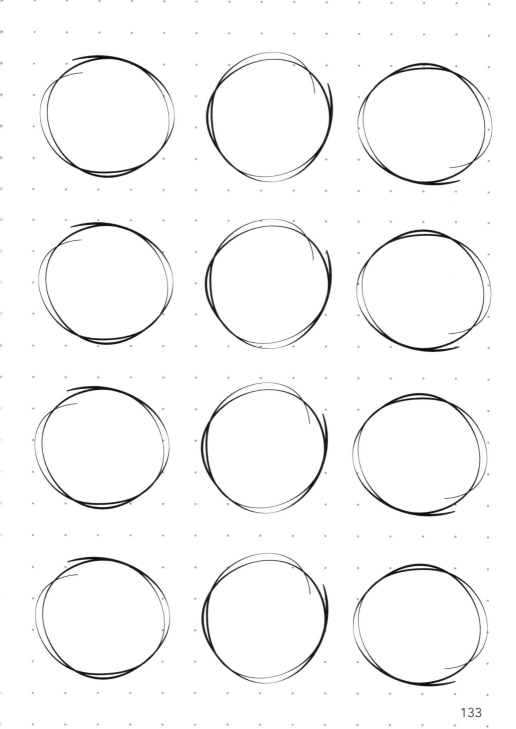

The
purpose
of life
is to
enjoy it.

THINK LESS, FEEL MORE.

Take Note of the Little Things

We're usually so caught up in our thinking that we pay little attention to our surroundings. This means we often overlook interesting details. From now on, encourage yourself to take

_____

_____

_____

_____

_____

_____

_____

_____

_____

_____

_____

_____

_____

_____

_____

_____

_____

note of the little things, such as what clothes a person is wearing, which flowers are beginning to bloom and what colour the walls around you are. You may be astonished at the number of things you have not noticed before.

Jot down all the little details you notice during an everyday trip outside, such as when you're running errands.

_____

_____

_____

_____

_____

_____

_____

_____

_____

_____

_____

_____

_____

_____

_____

_____

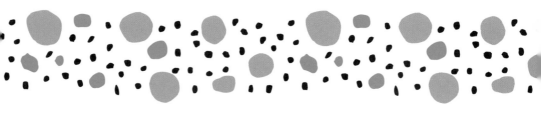

Moments of Beauty

Use mindfulness practice to notice the extraordinary and the beautiful in your day-to-day life.

Stop and smell the roses

Tuning into your senses can help you relish the present moment. Enjoy your sense of smell – rain-drenched earth, freshly baked bread, fresh fruit or barbecue smoke. Closing your eyes can sometimes help to heighten your appreciation.

Refreshing rain

If you usually avoid walking in the rain, don't! A walk in the rain can bring another dimension to your surroundings and there can be a heightened sense of smell, sound and feeling. As long as you have a warm place to dry out afterward, it can be refreshing and revitalizing, and can wash away any blues.

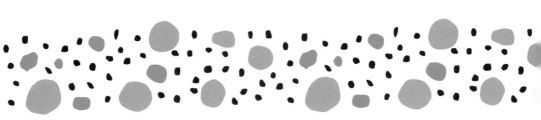

Urban beauty

When walking through a bustling city turn your eye to details – chimneys, rooftops, windows and the abundant variety of architectural features. Notice patterns – symmetry, circles, spirals, parallel lines, pairs and repetition. Allow your gaze to stay a moment in wonder as you appreciate the intricacy and beauty of the things humans have created.

Enchanted forests

Forests and woodlands are ideal places to go back to nature and to feel refreshed. Stand among the trees and soak up the peaceful atmosphere. Breathe in the forest smells: the wood's essential oils, moss and soil create magical aromas. Watch beams of light through the leaf canopy, enjoy the textures of rough bark and soft undergrowth, and look out for signs of insects and wildlife. This is something the whole family can relish, if you like – young children can run around, having make-believe adventures and discovering hiding places, while teenagers may be inspired to sit and write poetry or sketch plants and scenery. Don't forget to take a picnic to complete a memorable trip!

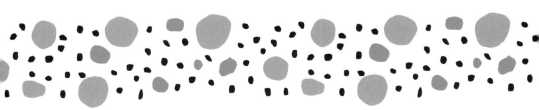

Everything you
do can be done
better from a place
of relaxation.

Stephen C. Paul

You must live in
the present, launch
yourself on every wave,
find your eternity
in each moment.

Henry David Thoreau

Garden Meditation

If you have your own garden, tune in to all your senses as you dig the soil and weed the flowerbeds, or simply sit and enjoy your lush, green surroundings. If you don't, visit a

public garden and pay full attention to the scents, the colours and shapes of your surroundings, and enjoy their beauty.

Every time you complete a garden meditation take a clipping from a plant or flower and stick it in one of the circles on these pages.

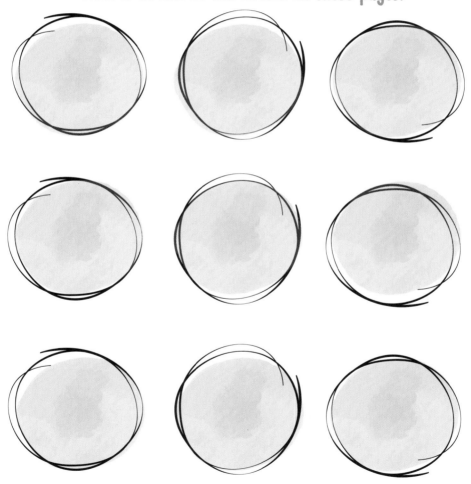

MINI MOMENTS
OF PEACE

Open up moments of calm
throughout your day. This
could be a few seconds spent
in quiet stillness while the kettle
boils or while your computer
is switching on, or it could
be as simple as taking a deep
breath of crisp morning air
as you leave the house.

You're only here
for a short visit.
Don't hurry,
don't worry.
And be sure to
smell the flowers
along the way.

Walter Hagen

WHEN IT'S TIME TO SEE A DOCTOR

If you've given everything else a try and a worried mind is still proving too much for you, it could be time to seek professional help. Go to your GP first and see what they suggest – they may recommend seeing a therapist, someone you can talk to about your concerns; or cognitive behavioural therapy; or even medication. Remember to be honest with your doctor – try not to hold back, and give as much detail as possible – and they'll be able to suggest the right solution for you and your worries. Complementary therapies can help a great deal to reduce the stresses and strains that could be causing you to feel unbalanced or stressed but sometimes, professional help is what's needed. You'll be on the right track and in safe hands, and will feel the benefit before you know it.

WE HOPE YOU ENJOY THE JOURNEY TOWARD A NEW, MORE MINDFUL YOU!

Notes

Use the following notes and doodle
pages however you please!

Doodles

Notes

Doodles

Notes

Image Credits

If you're interested in finding out more about our books,
find us on Facebook at **Summersdale Publishers**,
follow us on Twitter at **@Summersdale** and follow
our Instagram **@summersdalepublishers**.

Thanks very much for buying this Summersdale book.

www.summersdale.com